"Retro was never hotter than the mod decades when the men were 'mad' and the suits were plaid. These groovy gals and natty guys are the coolest cats around. Reeda Joseph, vintage archivist and collector of rarities, has gathered up the very best the fifties and sixties have to offer, with images that'll knock your socks off and inspire you to turn up the Sinatra, mix some martinis, and offer up a toast to your favorite fellow."

—Varla Ventura,
author of *Wild Women Talk about Love*
and *Sheroes*

Man Candy

DISHY DUDES AND MOD MEN

by Reeda Joseph

Published in the United States by Viva Editions, an imprint of Cleis Press, Inc., 2246 Sixth St., Berkeley, CA 94710.

Printed in China.
Cover and text design: Frank Wiedemann
All photography: Wright Card Co.
First Edition 10 9 8 7 6 5 4 3 2 1

Hardcover ISBN: 978-1-936740-68-0
E-book ISBN: 978-1-936740-75-8

Library of Congress Cataloging-in-Publication Data available on request.

For Tim Wright, of Wright Card Co.,
whose one-of-a-kind wit and sharp eye improve my work every day

and

To Nicolas Sherman, vivacious wordsmith

Ladies,

In this gluten-free, low-carb world, gals like you long for and need a little stress-reducing treat. You deserve some *Man Candy!* And while this confection has zero calories, it is plenty sweet. Way before there was "porn for women," there were dreamboats and stylin' studs aplenty who dressed to impress. I'm sorry, but a guy washing dishes or vacuuming is not enough for me. In these pages, there are dishy dudes, boss bosses, military men, beach bums, and boys next door who are happy to please YOU.

    I've been selecting these images for years, but here, I decided to share my own special secret collection of goodies with you, my fellow aficionados of the finer things in life. I left no stone unturned, and no church bazaar, garage sale, or fancy flea market escaped my search for the coolest images of men from back in the day. These groovy guys, hip cats, jivey-leaguers, beatniks, and flipniks will soon have you picking up bongos and twisting the night away!

Your gal pal,

Reeda

PERFECTION:

Now
available
in blue.

MEANWHI

LE,

at the James Bond casting party...

Betty and I are going to the school dance on Saturday. Are you? It'll be a gas!

Men:

If anything, they
can always carry
our stuff.

So, Fred, tell us more about this...Internet.

So...
you like the Beatles?

Are you from the future?

'Cause you look like part of mine.

They don't make them quite like they used to!

Men don't always share their feelings, so it's all the more juicy when they do!

Candles turn a microwave dinner into a meal at a five-star restaurant.

Men crave
freedom
almost as
much as they
crave us!

Almost...

Sometimes, the clothes do make the man!

Handsome
stands the
test of time.

Short shorts,
however. . .

Badminton
played in
loafers...
it was a
different
time then.

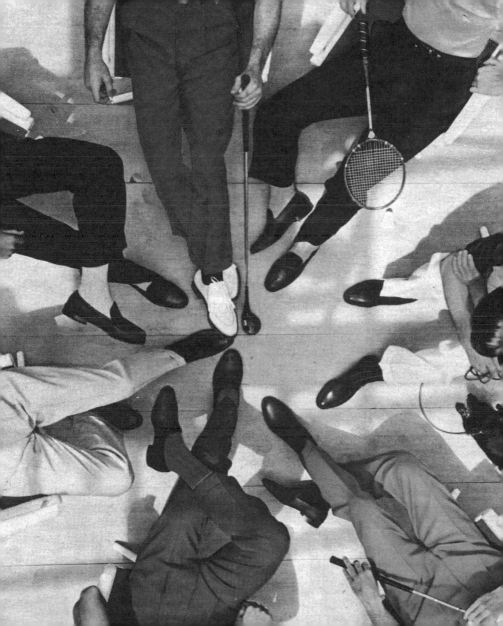

OF COURSE
HE'S GOING
TO SPEND
THAT
MONEY ON
YOU!

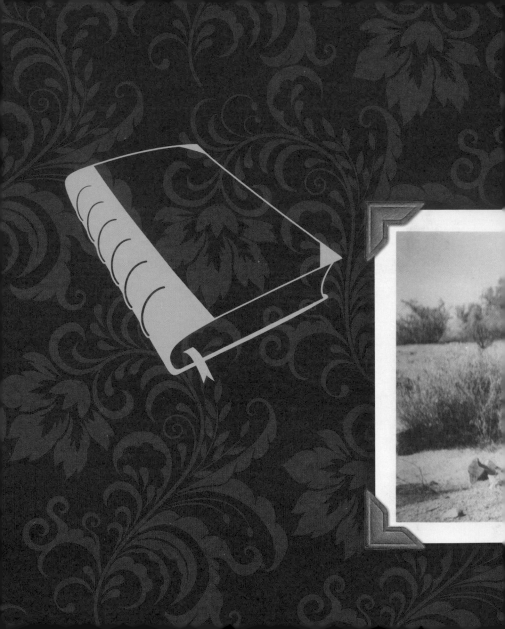

Put a book in his hand and you
get the best of both worlds!

Oh my god, look at his HAT!

Eat your
heart out,
Mad Men.

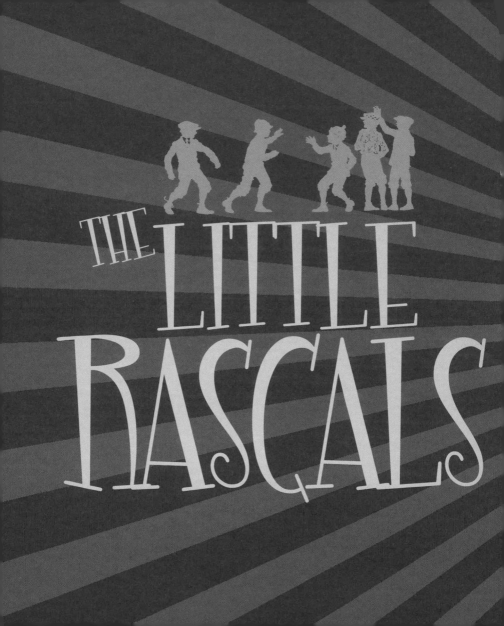

became
the big ones.

Can you reach into my front pocket and grab my wrench?

Who needs 20/20 vision when you look this good?

Hey Stud!

If you can't
afford a suit,
no clothing at all
is almost just
as good.

WOULD YOU LIKE to go steady WITH ME?

People will still think I'm cool in fifty years, *right*?

If you're trying to determine how normal we are, don't look at my wife's haircut.

WARNING
LADIES

It's the charming and handsome ones who can be the most trouble.

EVERYONE KNOWS...

there's a fabulous woman behind every great man!

I like two kinds of men

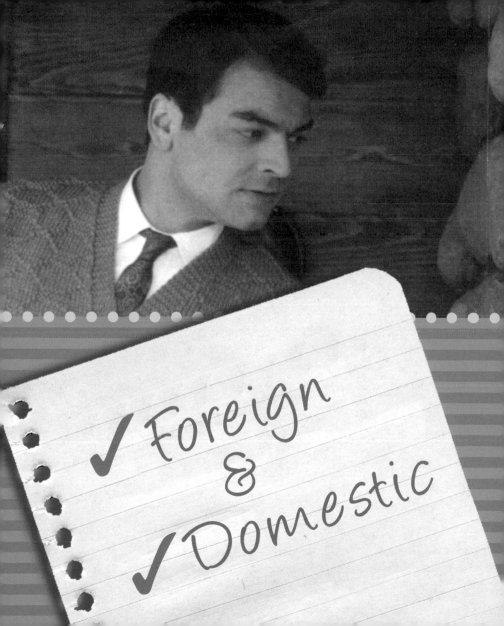

You like
what you
see?

Marry a nerd...
they're the
best-kept secret!

Oh, hello.
I didn't see
you there.

This guy is smoking—

SMOKING HOT,

that is.

There's nothing quite like catching a guy looking at you.

About the Author

Reeda Joseph has been a collector of one-of-a-kind nostalgic items since childhood. From church basements to estate sales to flea markets coast-to-coast, Reeda is constantly searching for (and finding) vintage images. A designer of cards and stationery for WrightCardCo.com, she lives in San Francisco, California.